BOOK • VIDEO

ADRIAN LEGG

FINGER-PICKING AND OPEN TUNINGS

CONTENTS

To access video visit:
www.halleonard.com/mylibrary

"Enter Code"
3273-3978-7953-1451

ISBN: 978-1-5400-7197-2

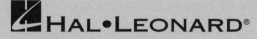

HAL•LEONARD®

Visit Hal Leonard Online at
www.halleonard.com

Contact us:
Hal Leonard
7777 West Bluemound Road
Milwaukee, WI 53213
Email: info@halleonard.com

In Europe, contact:
Hal Leonard Europe Limited
42 Wigmore Street
Marylebone, London, W1U 2RN
Email: info@halleonardeurope.com

In Australia, contact:
Hal Leonard Australia Pty. Ltd.
4 Lentara Court
Cheltenham, Victoria, 3192 Australia
Email: info@halleonard.com.au

BIOGRAPHY

Guitarist Adrian Legg was born in a Salvation Army hospital in London, England. In his school years, he studied oboe under parental pressure but began fashioning his own "guitars" from wood scraps and wire based on newspaper pictures.

Legg later was introduced to country music in Liverpool and worked there for two years before returning to London, where he played electric guitar in clubs and joined various bands that toured in and outside the U.K. A demand from a bandleader that he use an acoustic guitar up against a microphone to play loud chords for one number pushed Legg toward the acoustic as a separate instrument.

From there, Legg worked his way to being the acoustic virtuoso that he is today. Since the 1990 release of his first U.S. recording, *Guitars and Other Cathedrals*, Legg has more than lived up to the high expectations that come with praise from music critics, fans, and peers.

Guitars and Other Cathedrals was the first of five albums that Legg recorded for Relativity Records. His 1993 release, *Wine, Women, and Waltz*, was selected by the readers of *Guitar Player* magazine as "Best Overall Guitar Album" in their 1994 Reader's Poll. Legg also earned "Best Acoustic Album" from the same poll in 1992 for *Guitar For Mortals*, and in 1993 for *Mrs. Crowe's Blue Waltz*.

From 1993 to 1996, those same readers dubbed Legg as "Best Fingerstyle Guitarist," while the readers of *Guitarist* magazine published in England voted him "Acoustic Guitarist of the Decade."

Over the years, Legg has played the Montreux Jazz Festival and toured with the likes of Richard Thompson, David Lindley, Joe Satriani, and Eric Johnson, joining the latter two along with Steve Vai for the renowned G3 Tour in 1996 and 1997.

In 2004, Legg released *Inheritance* on Vai's Favored Nations label. Here, Legg contrasts raw, swampy blues with wistful grace and tells remarkable family histories as in the moody atmospheres of "The Good Soldier," which is an ode to his grandfather, who was blinded during World War I. Elsewhere on the album, gentle ballads, snappy percussive jams, and rock-edged electricity blend with hints of folk music, Irish jigs, and traditional church music.

But as popular as his catalog of recordings is, Legg's true home is on the stage. "Playing live is the whole point," he has said. "Everyone makes a journey, an effort. We all come together—me, the audience, the people who run the venue—to share this wonderful, universal human emotional interaction. This is where music lives."

SELECT DISCOGRAPHY

Requiem for a Hick (Westwood, 1977)

Techno Picker (Spindrift, 1983)

Fretmelt (Spindrift, 1984)

Lost for Words (1986)

Guitars and Other Cathedrals (Relativity, 1990)

Guitar for Mortals (Relativity, 1992)

Wine, Women, and Waltz (Relativity, 1993)

Mrs. Crowe's Blue Waltz (Relativity, 1993)

High Strung Tall Tales (Relativity, 1994)

Waiting for a Dancer (Red House, 1997)

Fingers and Thumbs (Red House, 1999)

Guitar Bones (2002)

Inheritance (Favored Nations, 2004)

Slow Guitar (2011)

Dead Bankers (2014)

SUGGESTED LISTENING

James Burton *Corn Pickin' and Slick Slidin'* (See for Miles, 1969)

Eric Johnson *Ah Via Musicom* (Capitol, 1990)

G3 *G3 Live in Concert* (Sony, 1997)

Adrian Legg *Guitars and Other Cathedrals (Relativity, 1990);
Inheritance* (Favored Nations, 2004)

GUITAR NOTATION LEGEND

Guitar music can be notated three different ways: on a *musical staff*, in *tablature*, and in *rhythm slashes*.

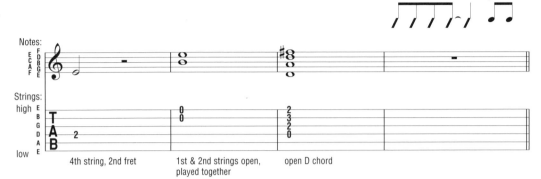

RHYTHM SLASHES are written above the staff. Strum chords in the rhythm indicated. Use the chord diagrams found at the top of the first page of the transcription for the appropriate chord voicings. Round noteheads indicate single notes.

THE MUSICAL STAFF shows pitches and rhythms and is divided by bar lines into measures. Pitches are named after the first seven letters of the alphabet.

TABLATURE graphically represents the guitar fingerboard. Each horizontal line represents a string, and each number represents a fret.

4th string, 2nd fret | 1st & 2nd strings open, played together | open D chord

---

HALF-STEP BEND: Strike the note and bend up 1/2 step.

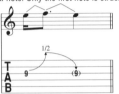

WHOLE-STEP BEND: Strike the note and bend up one step.

GRACE NOTE BEND: Strike the note and immediately bend up as indicated.

SLIGHT (MICROTONE) BEND: Strike the note and bend up 1/4 step.

BEND AND RELEASE: Strike the note and bend up as indicated, then release back to the original note. Only the first note is struck.

PRE-BEND: Bend the note as indicated, then strike it.

VIBRATO: The string is vibrated by rapidly bending and releasing the note with the fretting hand.

WIDE VIBRATO: The pitch is varied to a greater degree by vibrating with the fretting hand.

HAMMER-ON: Strike the first (lower) note with one finger, then sound the higher note (on the same string) with another finger by fretting it without picking.

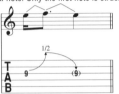

PULL-OFF: Place both fingers on the notes to be sounded. Strike the first note and without picking, pull the finger off to sound the second (lower) note.

LEGATO SLIDE: Strike the first note and then slide the same fret-hand finger up or down to the second note. The second note is not struck.

SHIFT SLIDE: Same as legato slide, except the second note is struck.

TRILL: Very rapidly alternate between the notes indicated by continuously hammering on and pulling off.

TAPPING: Hammer ("tap") the fret indicated with the pick-hand index or middle finger and pull off to the note fretted by the fret hand.

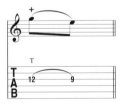

NATURAL HARMONIC: Strike the note while the fret-hand lightly touches the string directly over the fret indicated.

PINCH HARMONIC: The note is fretted normally and a harmonic is produced by adding the edge of the thumb or the tip of the index finger of the pick hand to the normal pick attack.

PICK SCRAPE: The edge of the pick is rubbed down (or up) the string, producing a scratchy sound.

MUFFLED STRINGS: A percussive sound is produced by laying the fret hand across the string(s) without depressing, and striking them with the pick hand.

PALM MUTING: The note is partially muted by the pick hand lightly touching the string(s) just before the bridge.

RAKE: Drag the pick across the strings indicated with a single motion.

TREMOLO PICKING: The note is picked as rapidly and continuously as possible.

VIBRATO BAR DIVE AND RETURN: The pitch of the note or chord is dropped a specified number of steps (in rhythm), then returned to the original pitch.

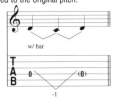

VIBRATO BAR SCOOP: Depress the bar just before striking the note, then quickly release the bar.

VIBRATO BAR DIP: Strike the note and then immediately drop a specified number of steps, then release back to the original pitch.

Chapter 1: "Coging's Glory"

† DADGAD tuning, down 1/2 step:
(low to high) D♭-A♭-D♭-G♭-B♭-E♭

†Throughout Chapter 1

A

Fast ♩ = 144

*D7sus4

*Chord symbols reflect basic harmony.
**Rasgueado: strum in downward motion w/ nails of pick-hand fingers.

B

D7(no3rd)   D5

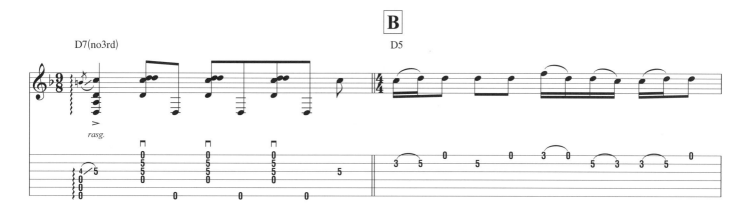

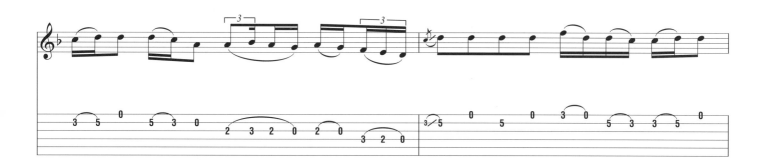

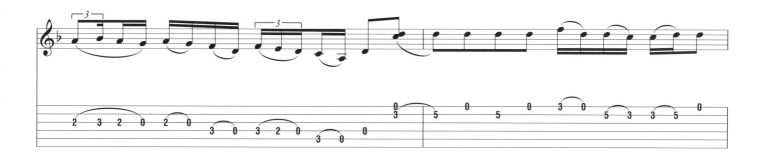

5

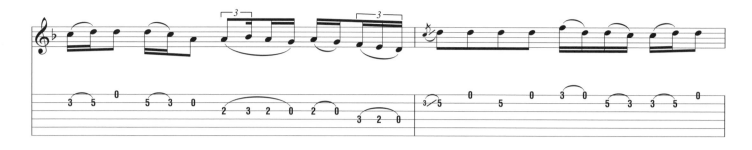

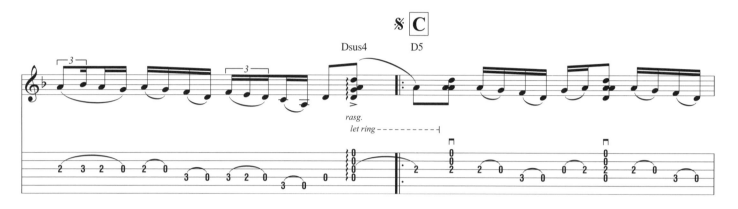

% C

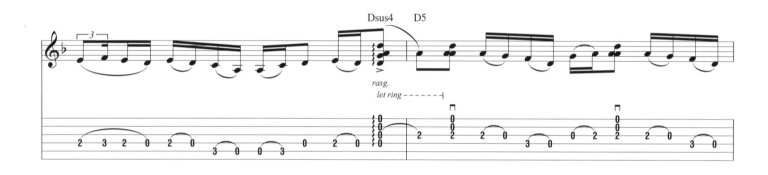

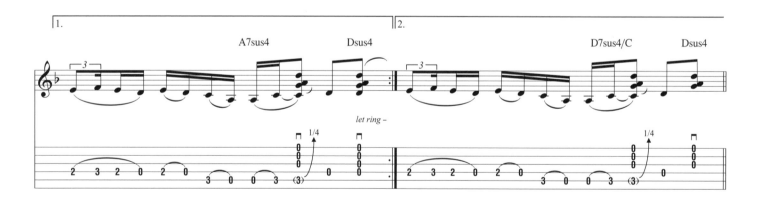

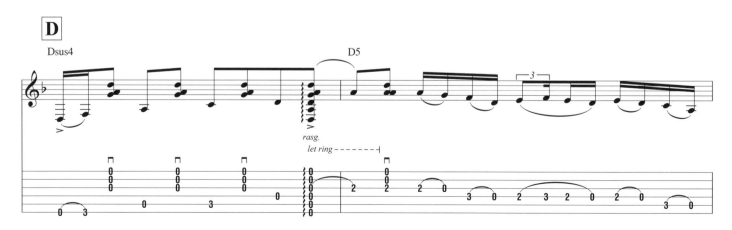

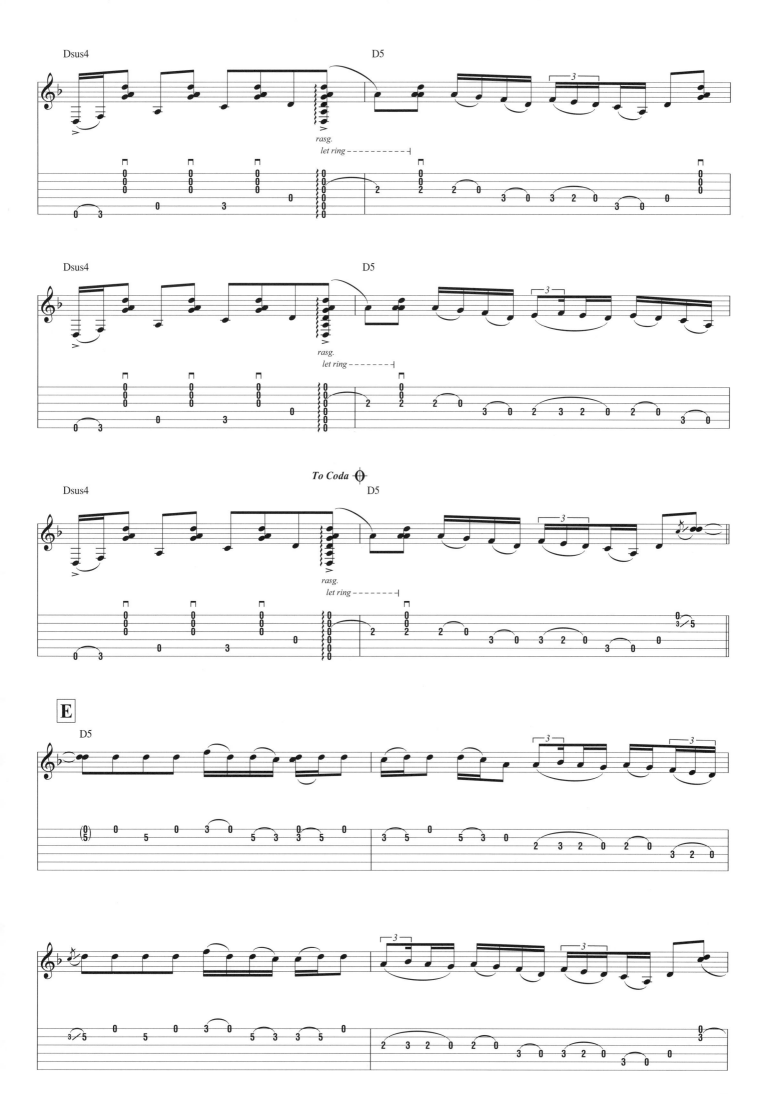

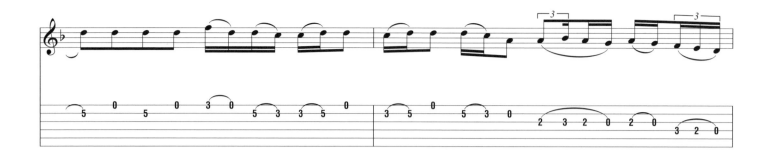

D.S. al Coda
(take repeats)

Coda

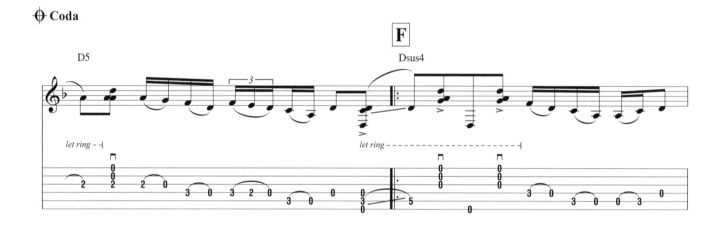

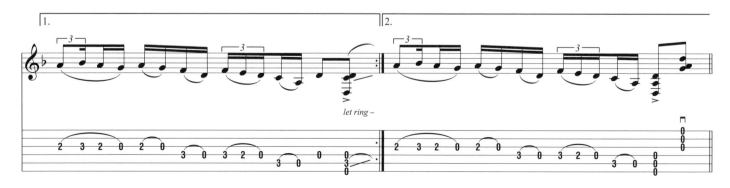

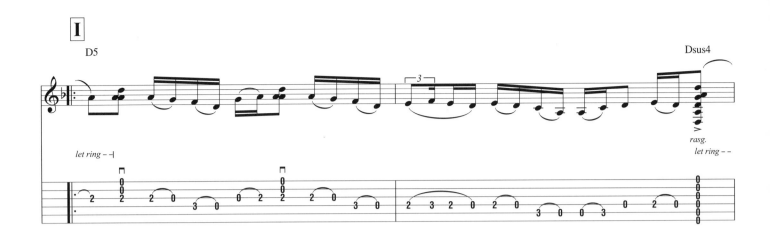

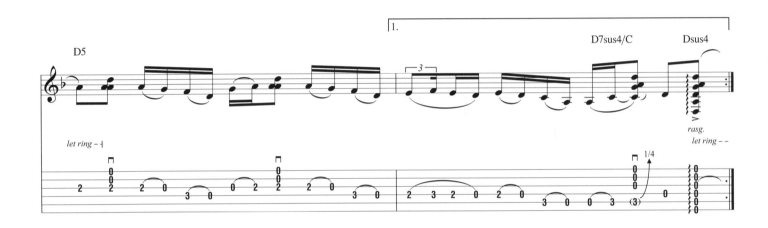

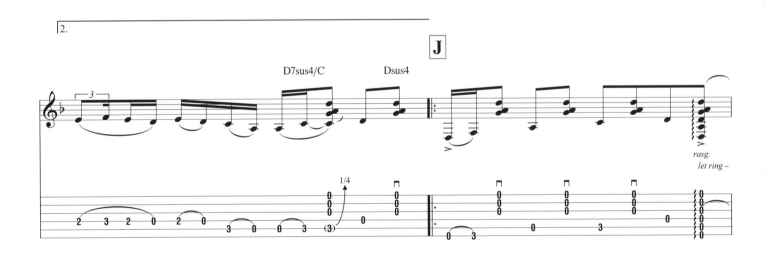

"Coging's Glory" Examples

Example 1
(5:44)

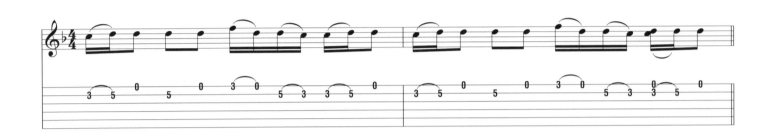

Example 2
(6:05)

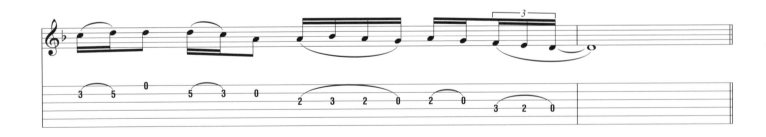

Example 3
(6:16)

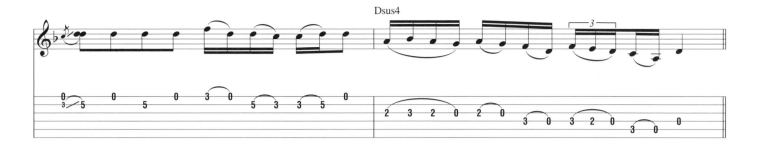

Example 4
(7:18)

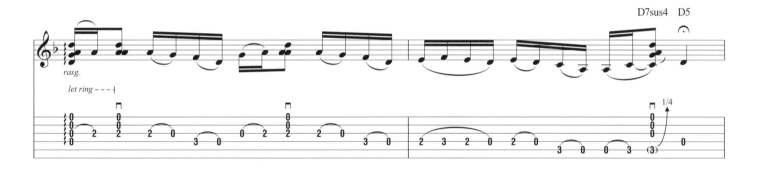

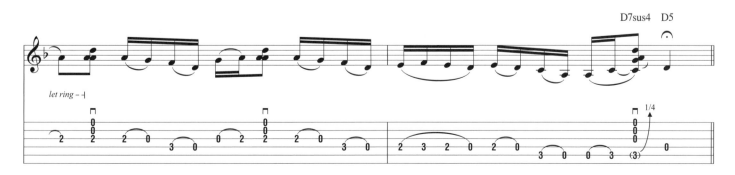

Example 5

(8:35)

D

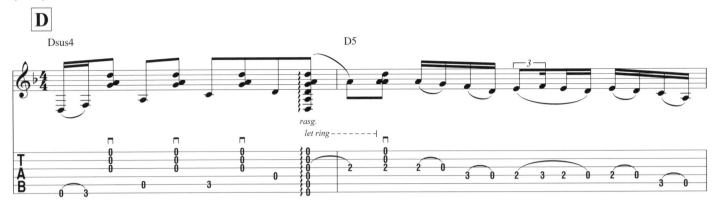

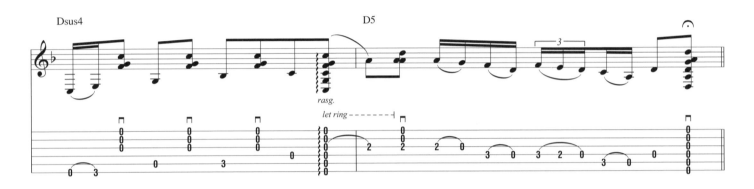

Example 6

(9:16)

F

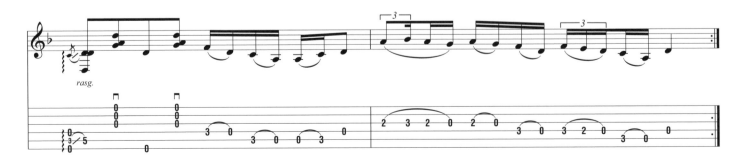

Example 7
(10:12)

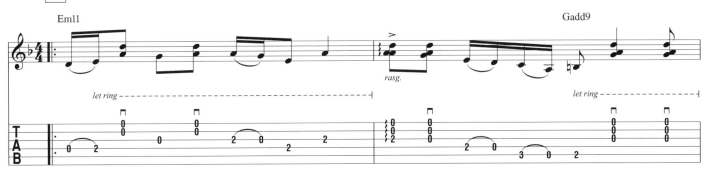

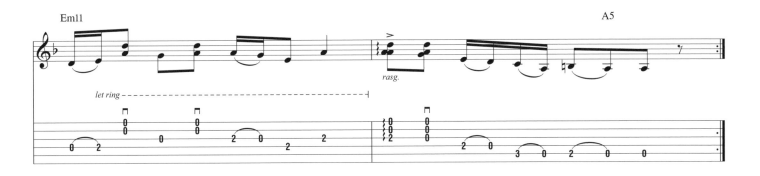

Example 8
(11:42)

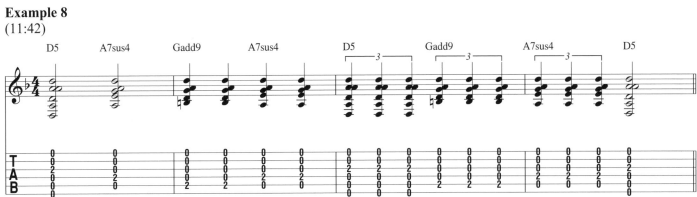

Chapter 2: "The Netsman and the Laird"

†DADGAD tuning, down 1/2 step:
(low to high) Db-Ab-Db-Gb-Ab-Db

†Throughout Chapter 2

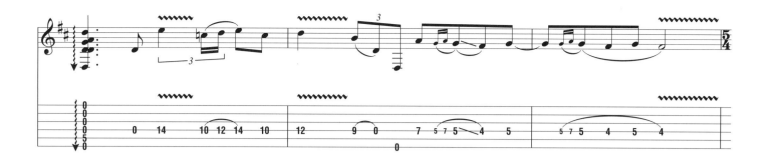

C

Faster ♩. = 140

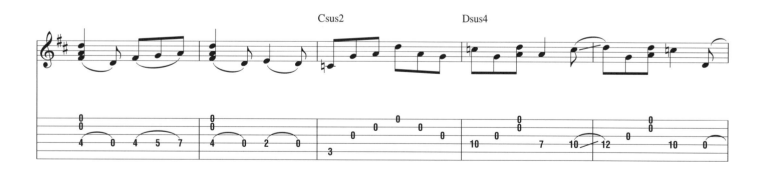

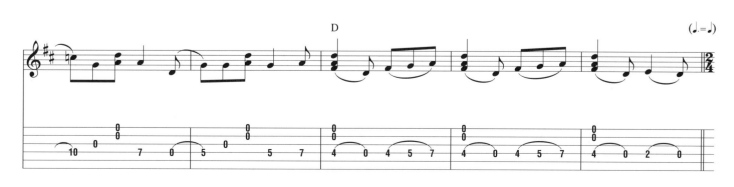

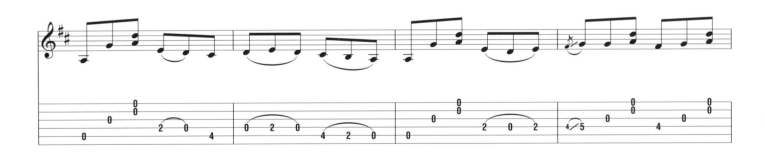

E

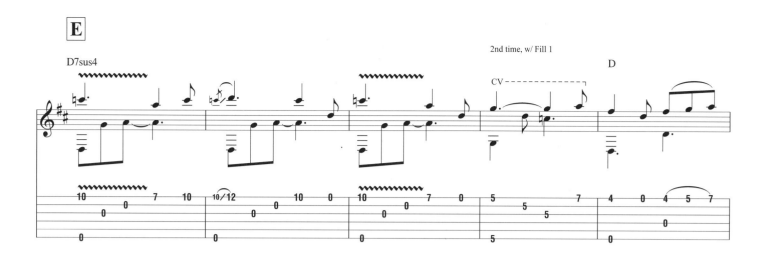

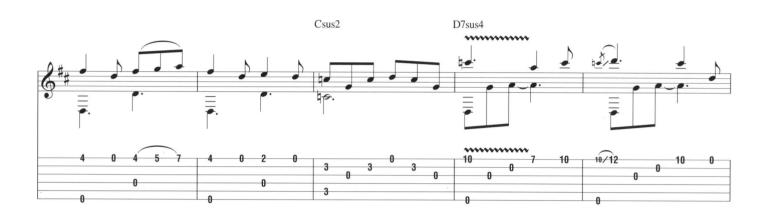

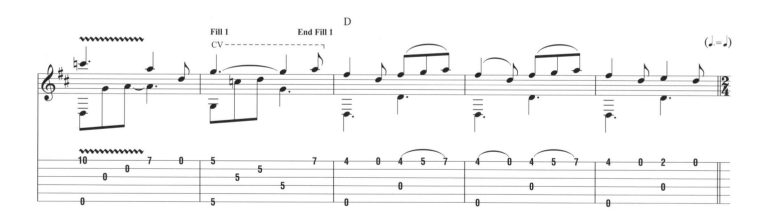

F

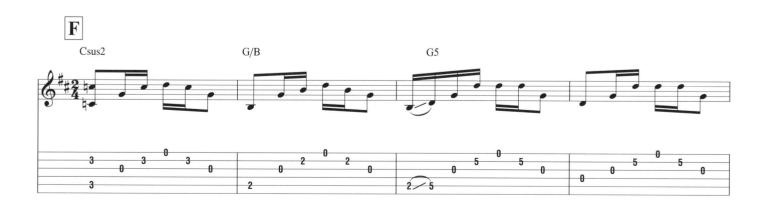

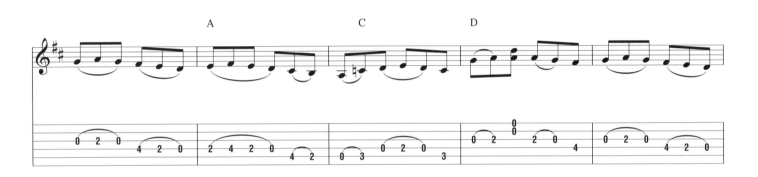

D.S. al Coda 1

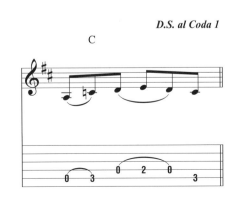

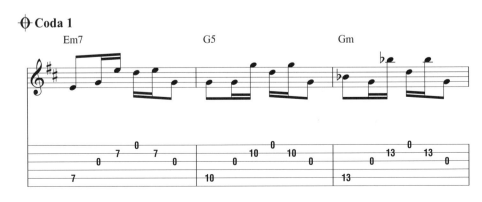

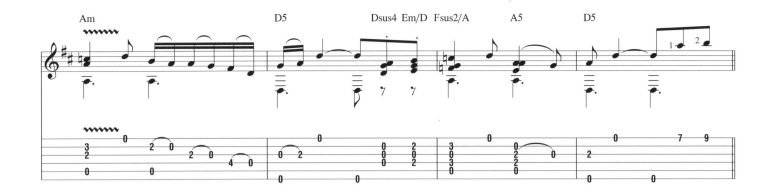

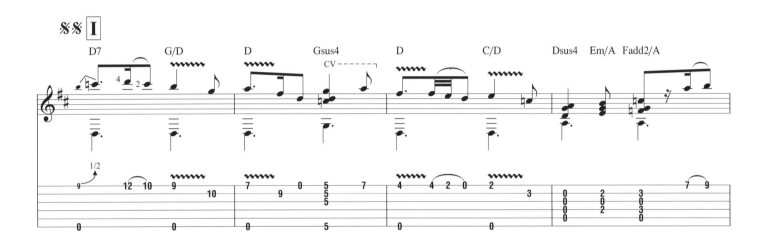

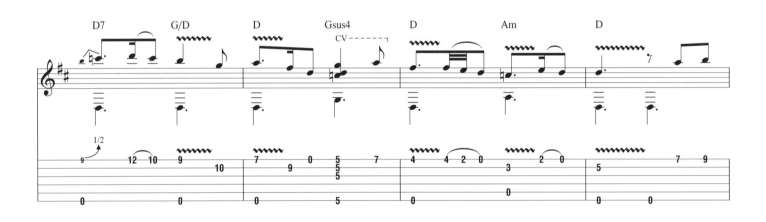

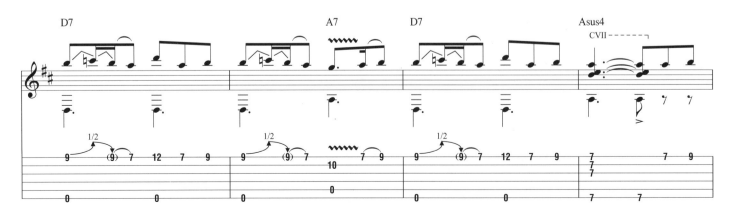

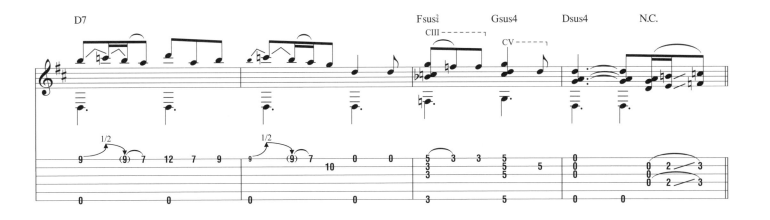

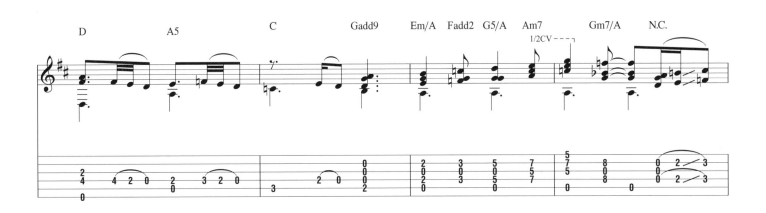

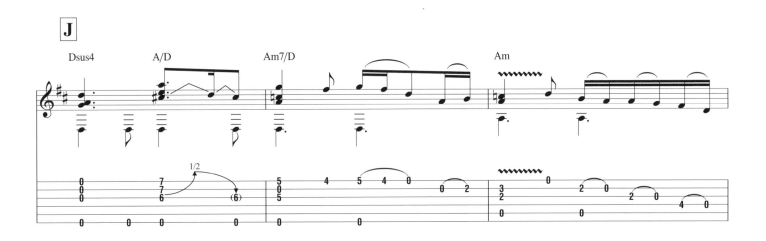

To Coda 2 ⊕

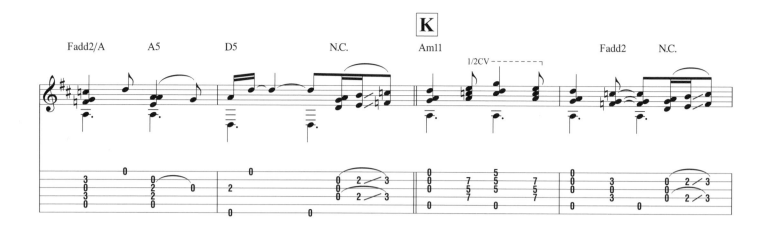

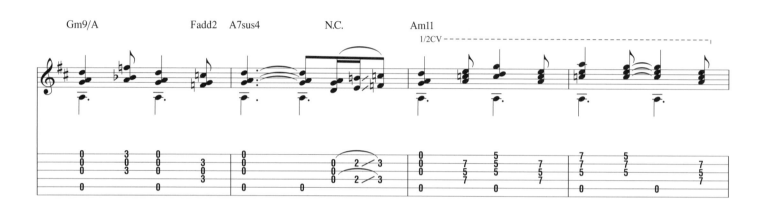

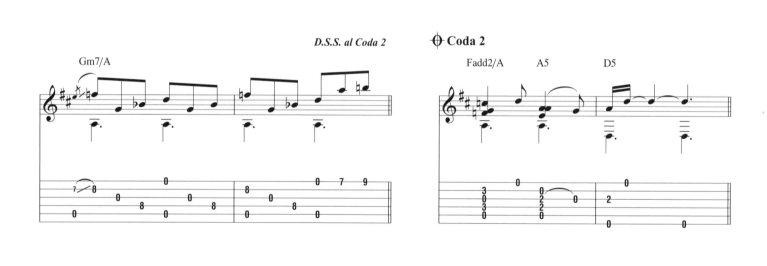

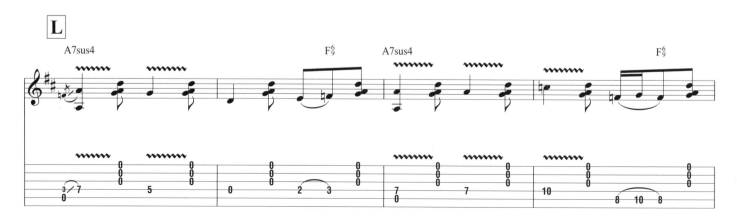

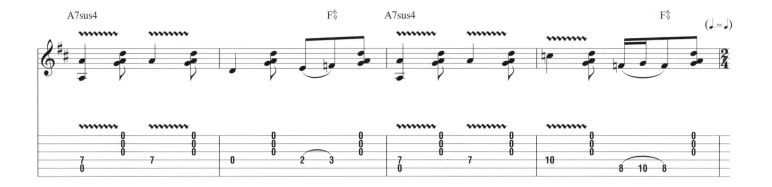

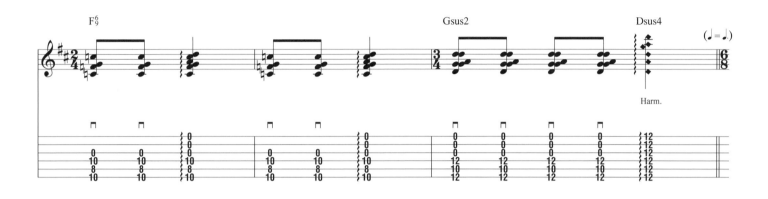

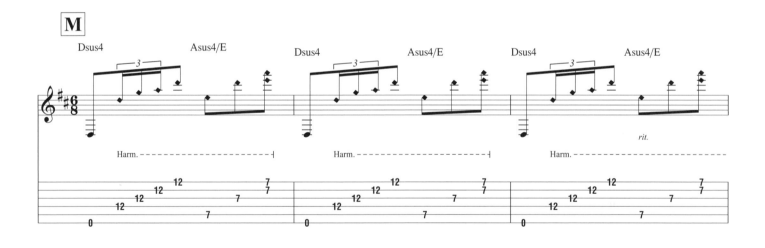

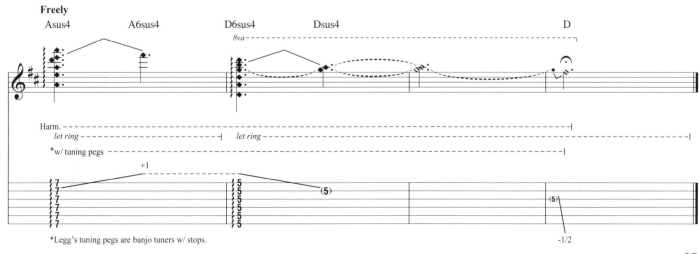

*Legg's tuning pegs are banjo tuners w/ stops.

"The Netsman and the Laird" Examples

Example 9
(8:00)

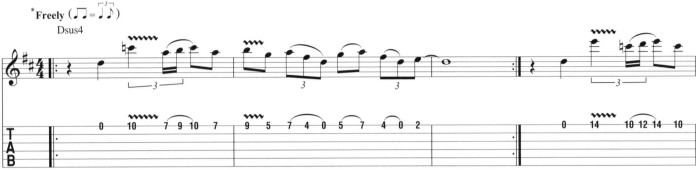

*Tempo, feel & time signatures of examples follow the tune.

Example 10 Main Theme
(9:12)

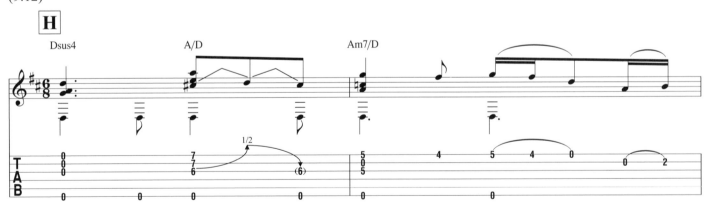

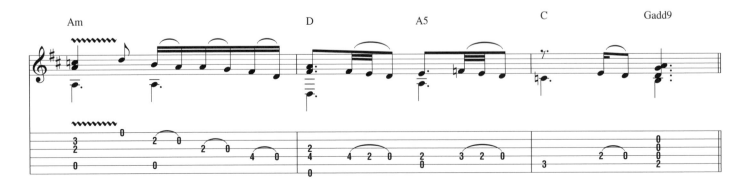

Example 11
(11:22)

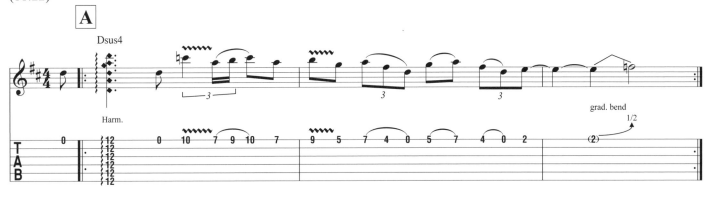

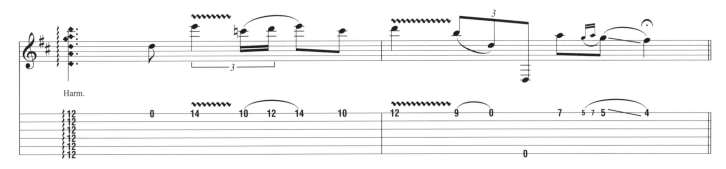

Example 12
(12:27)

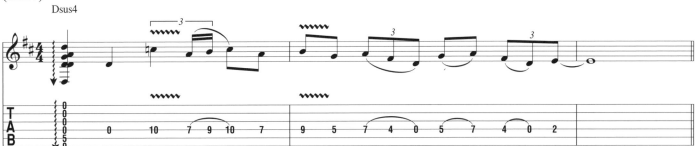

Example 13
(12:43)

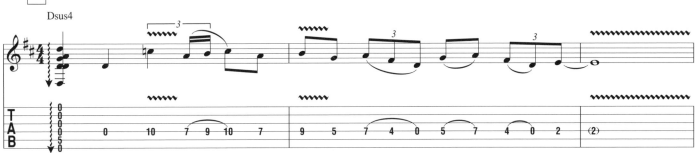

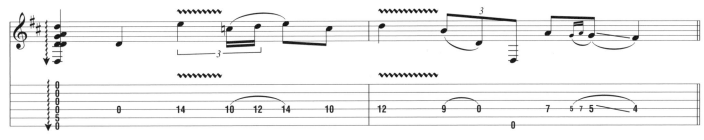

Example 14
(13:52)

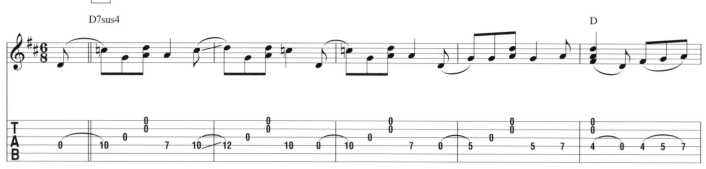

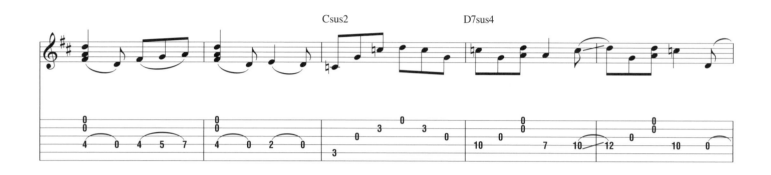

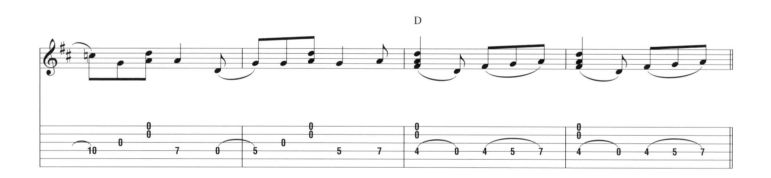

Example 15
(14:25)

Example 16
(14:50)

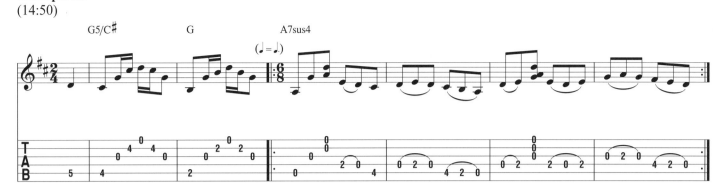

Example 17
(15:41)

Example 18
(16:15)

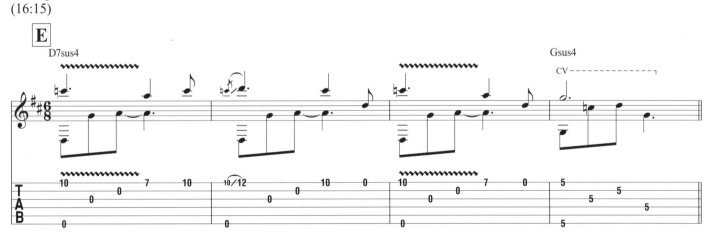

Example 19
(16:34)

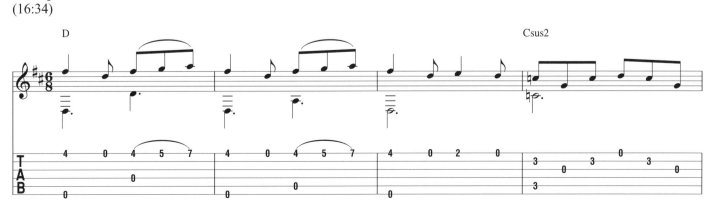

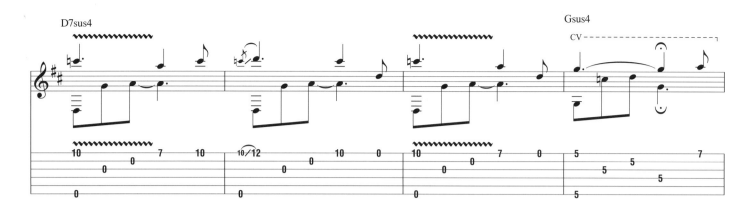

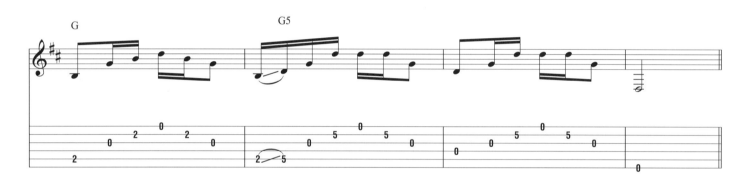

Example 20
(17:00)

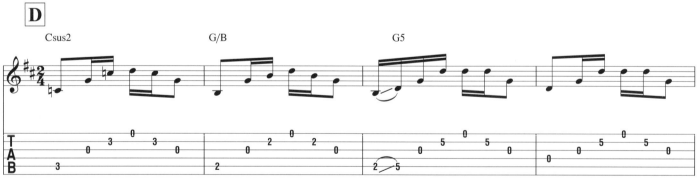

Example 21
(18:12)

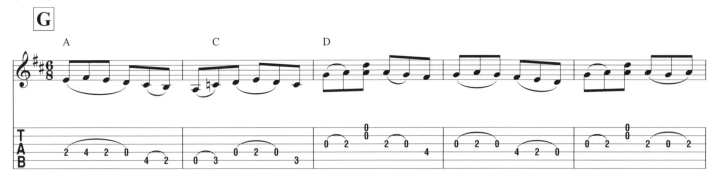

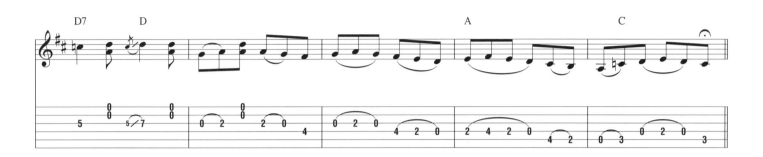

Example 22
(18:25)

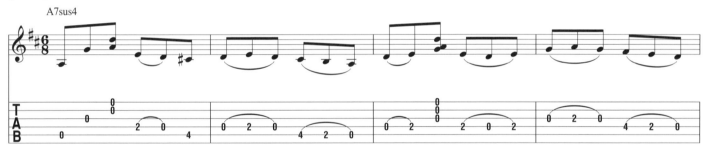

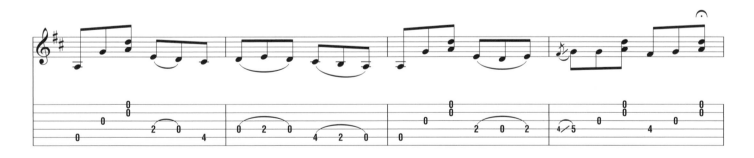

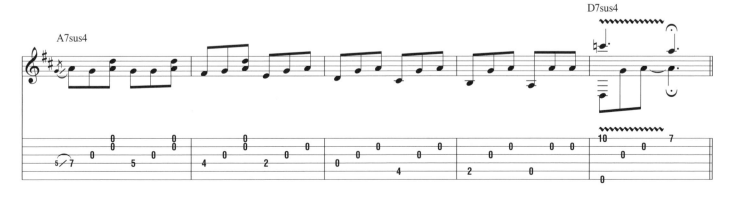

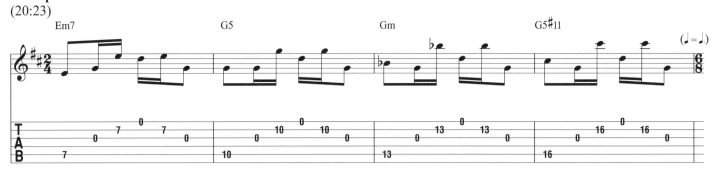

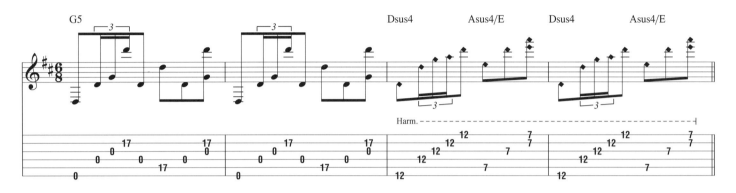

Example 24
(22:01)

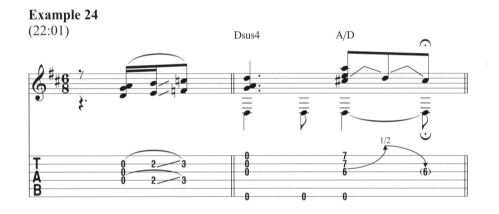

Example 25
(22:20)

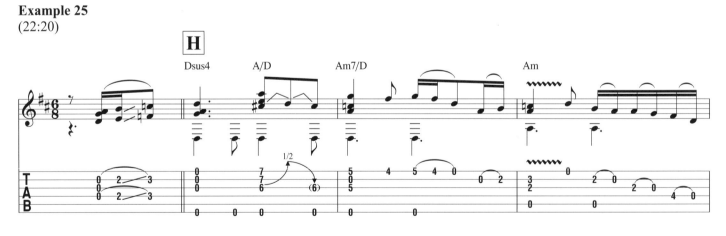

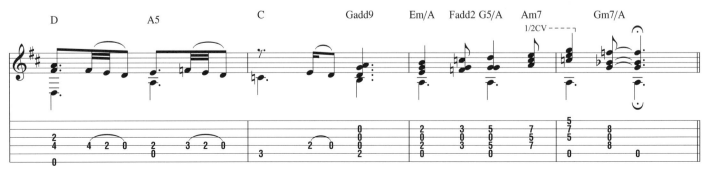

Example 26
(22:48)

Example 27
(25:19)

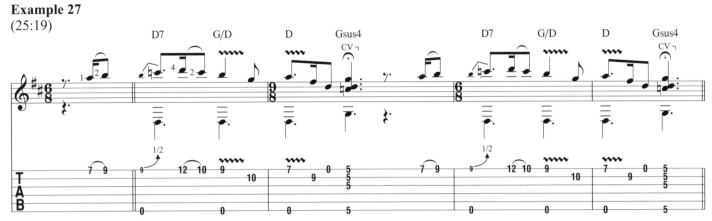

Example 28
(26:07)

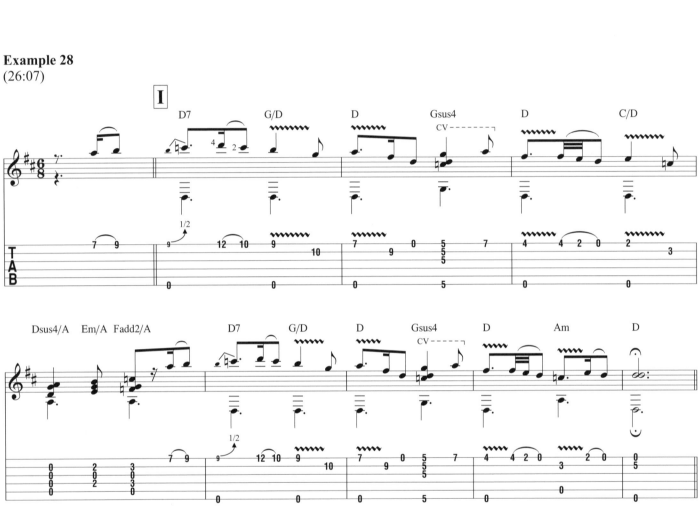

Example 29
(26:24)

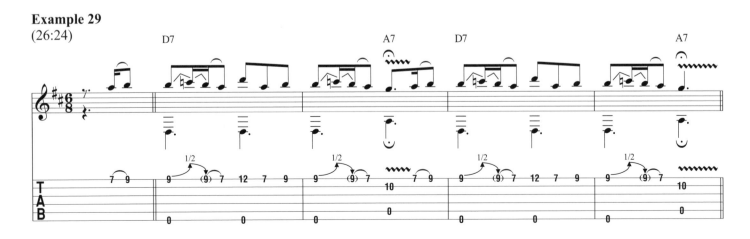

Example 30
(28:27)

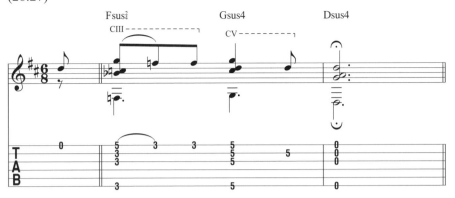

Example 31
(30:25)

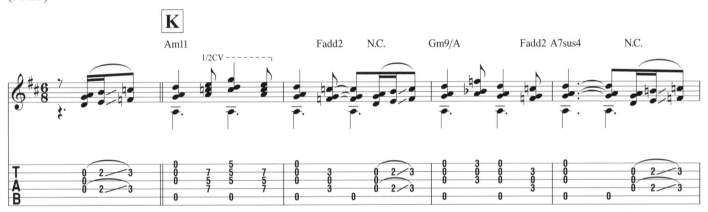

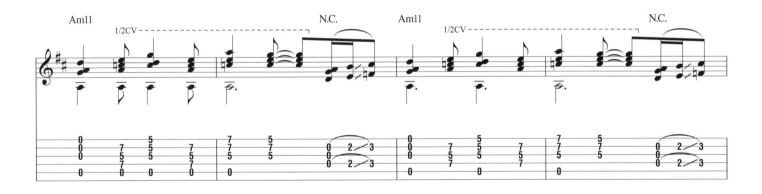

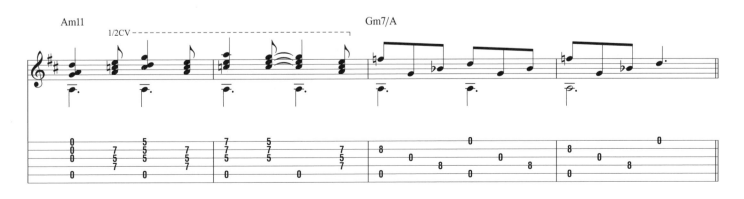

Example 32
(32:44)

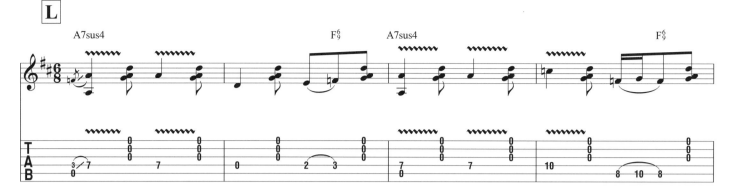

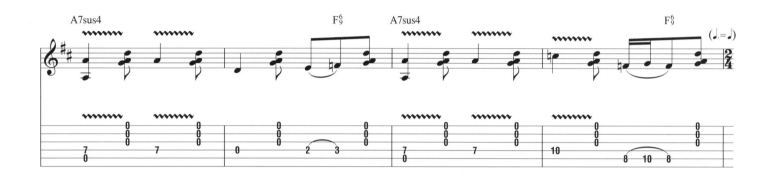

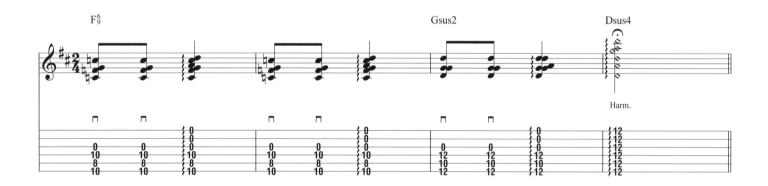

Example 33
(33:39)

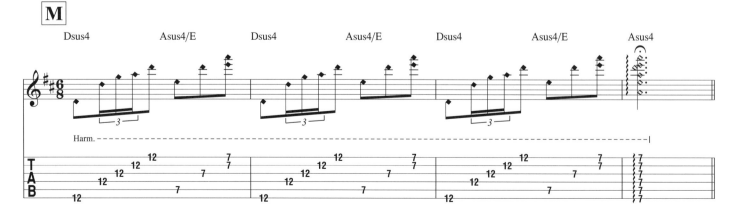

Chapter 3: "Sour Grapes"

†† Open G tuning, down 1/2 step:
(low to high) D♭-G♭-D♭-G♭-B♭-D♭

††Throughout Chapter 3

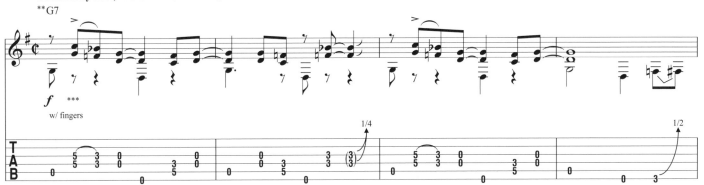

*Use swing eighths (♫ = ♩♪) throughout Chapter 3.
**Chord symbols reflect basic harmony.
***Downstemmed notes stopped from ringing
w/ heel of pickhand throughout.

†w/ tuning peg

†Legg's tuning pegs are
banjo tuners w/ stops.

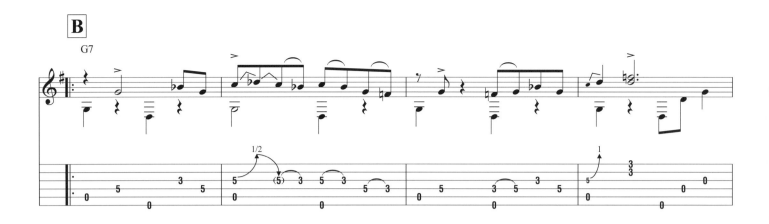

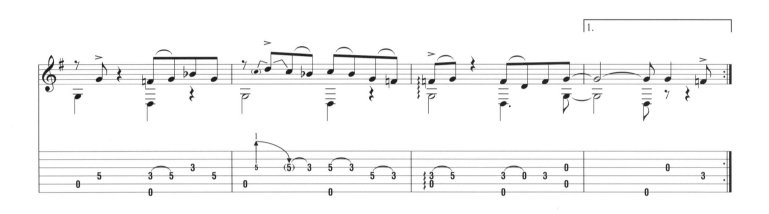

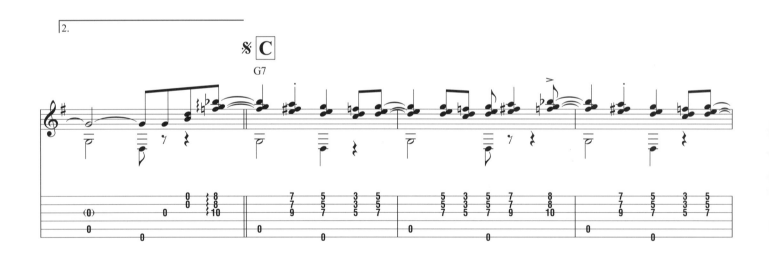

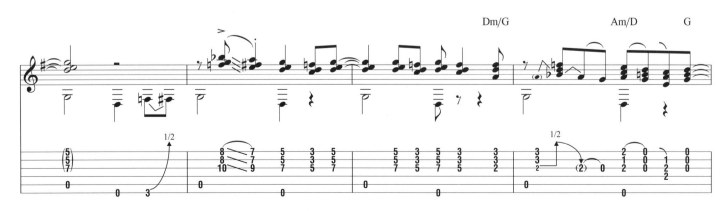

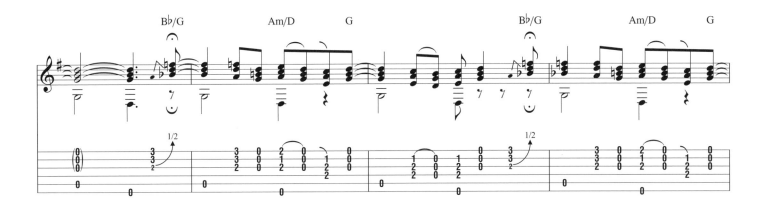

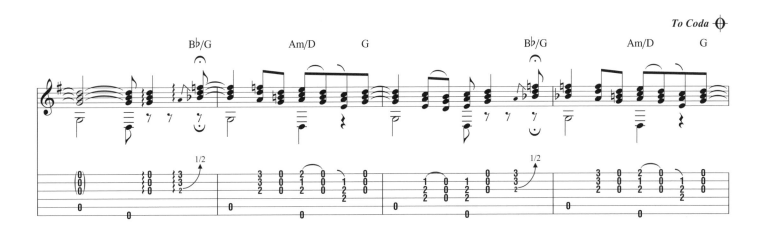

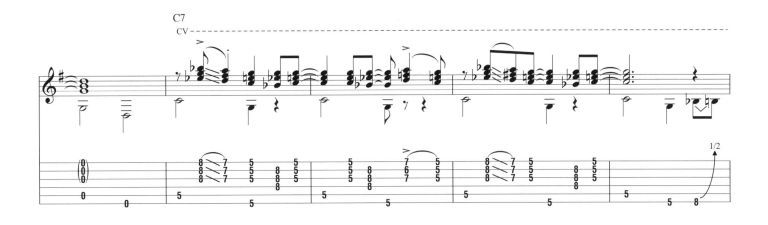

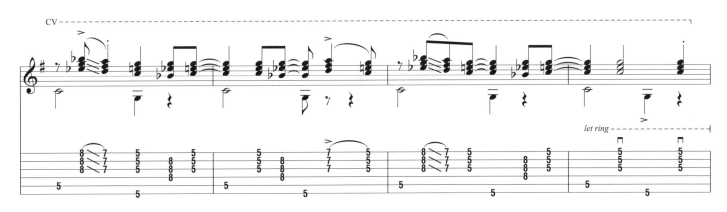

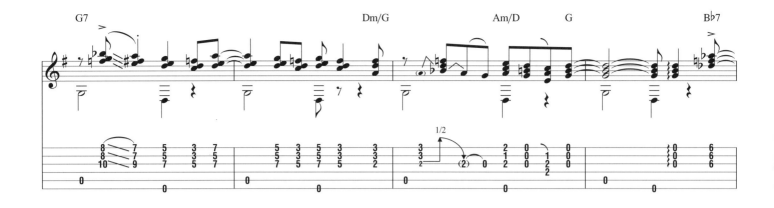

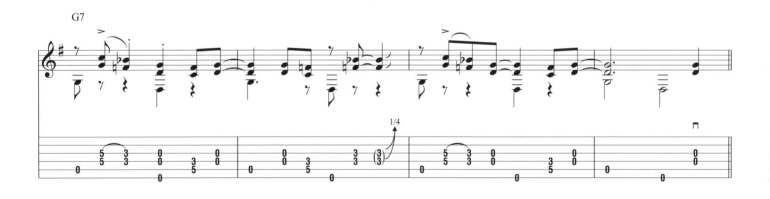

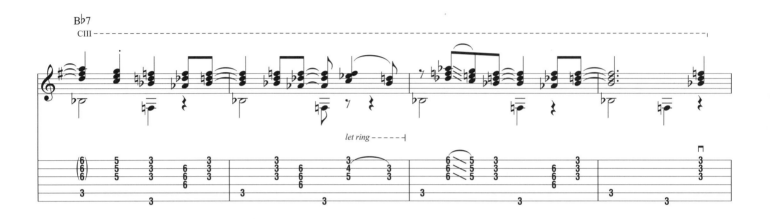

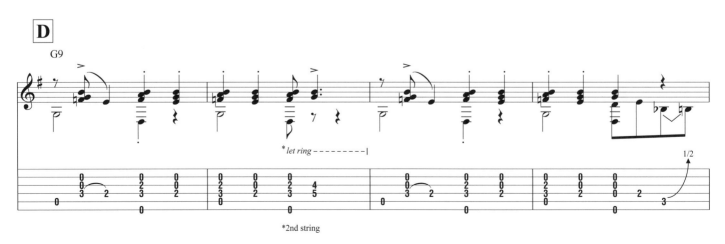

*2nd string

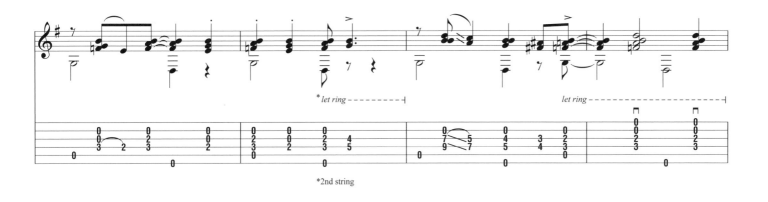

*2nd string

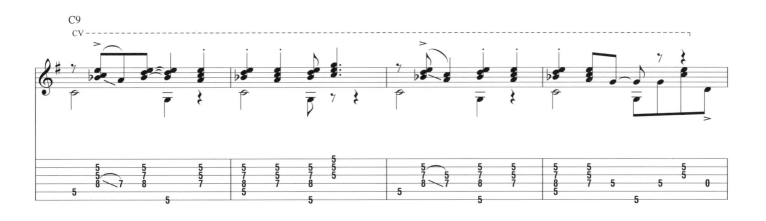

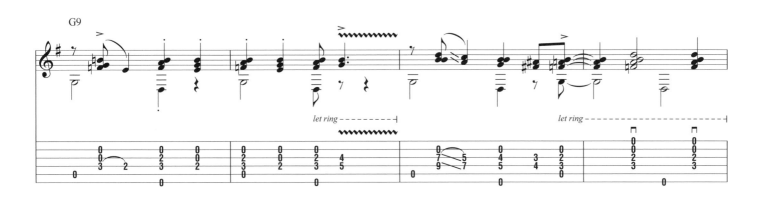

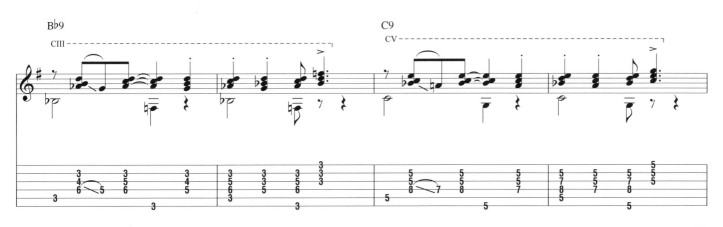

*let ring ---------|
**2nd string*

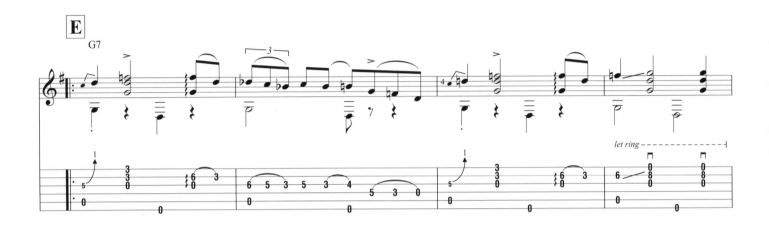

E G7

let ring --------------|

1.

let ring --------------|

2.

Coda

F

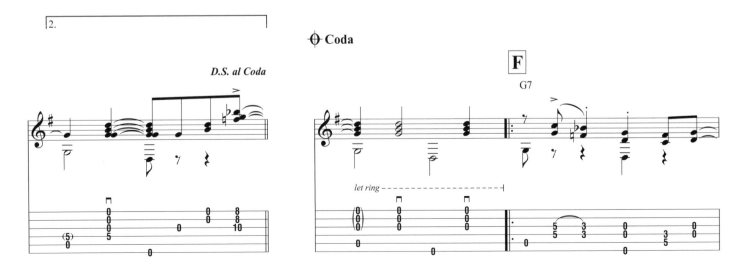

D.S. al Coda

G7

let ring --------------|

"Sour Grapes" Examples

Example 34
(9:42)

*Moderately slow, in 2   ♩ = 92

G7

*Tempo, feel & time signatures of examples follow the tune.

**Rhythmic variation compared to performance.

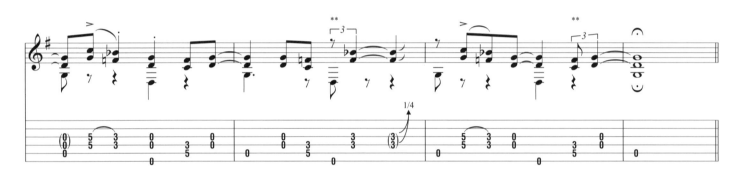

Example 35
(9:56)

C7/G

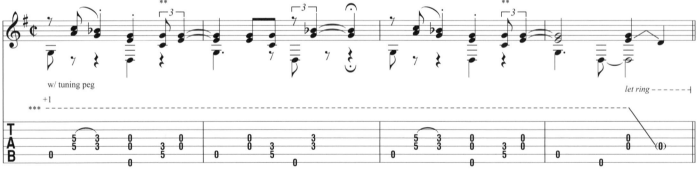

w/ tuning peg

let ring - - - - - -

***

***Tune 4th string up 1 step

Example 36
(10:18)

B

G7

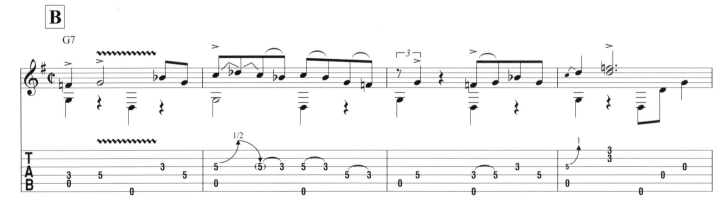

44

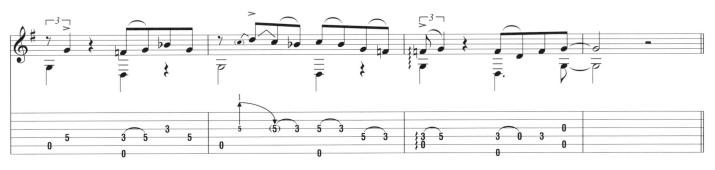

Example 37
(11:05)

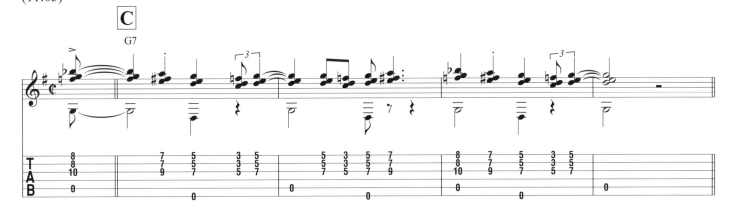

Example 38
(12:35)

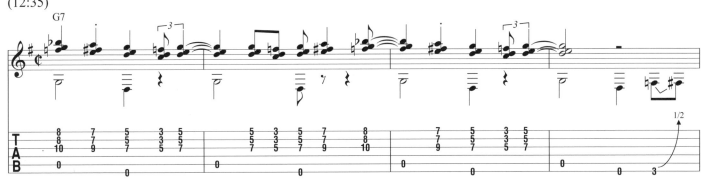

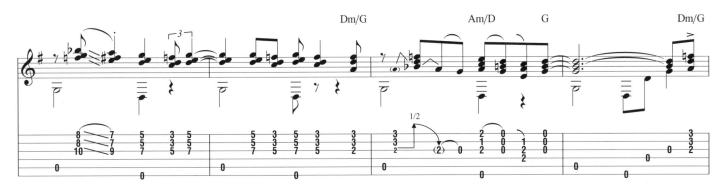

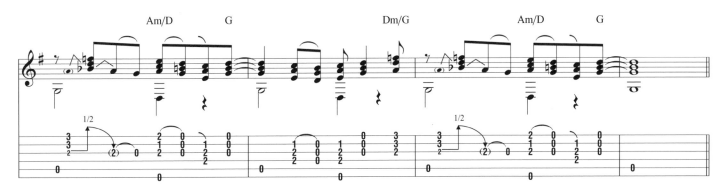

Example 39
(13:50)

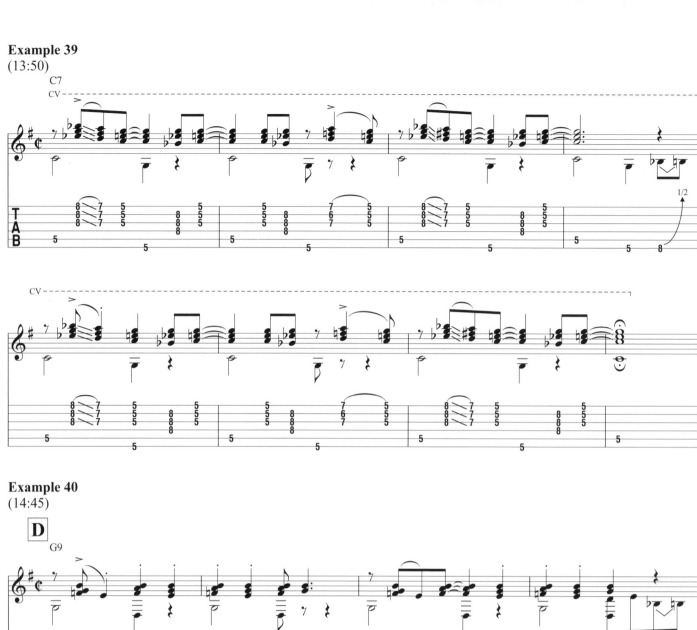

Example 40
(14:45)

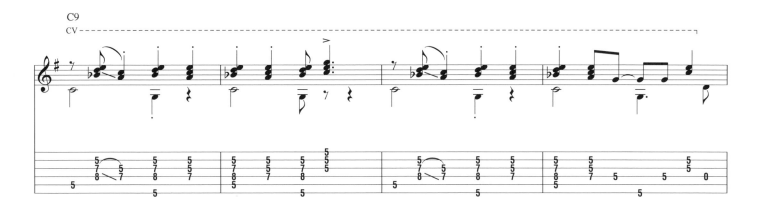

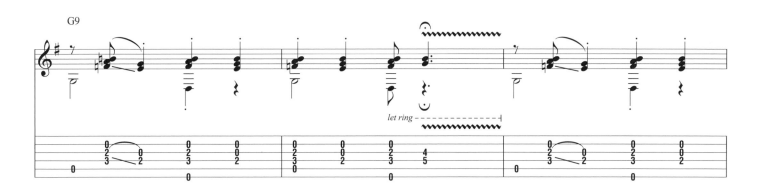

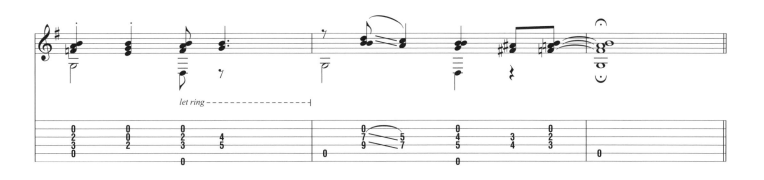

Example 41
(16:43)